Rocking Chair at the End of the World

poems by

Sarah Bokich

Finishing Line Press
Georgetown, Kentucky

Rocking Chair at the
End of the World

Copyright © 2017 by Sarah Bokich
ISBN 978-1-63534-175-1 First Edition
All rights reserved under International and Pan-American Copyright Conventions.
No part of this book may be reproduced in any manner whatsoever without written permission from the publisher, except in the case of brief quotations embodied in critical articles and reviews.

ACKNOWLEDGMENTS

My thanks to the editors of the following journals in which these poems first appeared:

VoiceCatcher: "Sailor"
Cloudbank: "If I ever allege you don't understand me, know—"
The Timberline Review: "In Good Voice"

Much gratitude to Dee W. Hock, Herman Asarnow, and Peter Sears, as well as The Attic Institute of Arts and Letters and Mountain Writers Series.

All my love to Manny and Bellamy.

Publisher: Leah Maines

Editor: Christen Kincaid

Cover Art: Red Scandal Graphics, www.redscandalgraphics.com

Author Photo: Damian Blacklock, damianblacklockphotography.com

Cover Design: Stephanie Layton

Printed in the USA on acid-free paper.
Order online: www.finishinglinepress.com
also available on amazon.com

Author inquiries and mail orders:
Finishing Line Press
P. O. Box 1626
Georgetown, Kentucky 40324
U. S. A.

Table of Contents

Trading the Animals 1
Sailor 2
Bread 3
The Visitors 4
Summer 5
The Birds Have Returned from Africa 6
The Last Time I Saw You 7
Hunger 8
Gods and Fathers 9
Prayer 10
In Praise of Fat Babies 11
Lucky Girl 12
Flourishing Desert 13
Ants 14
Betrayal 15
The Drive 16
If I ever allege you don't understand me, know— 18
Tour Guide 19
What Dying is Like 20
Baby Talks 21
Rocking Chair at the End of the World 22
In Good Voice 23

For Alice

Trading the Animals

You cannot buy puffins, no matter how much you want to.
Even sitting on a million dollars your zoo could still be
sans puffins. If you ask around though, someone might
trade you some for eight hundred bug-eyed mackerel.

You cannot sell an elephant, not even in Calgary
where he shouldn't be in the first place; he hates the cold
and the snowman the keeper built. Yet you can loan him
somewhere warm and hope for a decent trade.

They have a market price, of course, or else we wouldn't
find their bodies headless and scattered across the savannah.
But we are on the side of good, we pretend that lives
and money can be kept separate as lions and lambs.

So we play this game, trading jellyfish for snipe and chimps
for parrots, animals loaded onto trucks where water sloshes
inside tanks and damp noses sniff at the air vents of crates.
That's how we get around it, the puffinless zoos

and frostbitten feet, curating our collections without a dime.
But there is one more thing—lemurs. I'd love to see them
crouched, wringing their dark, graceful hands, but all I got
was an Indian rhino and three Komodo dragons.

Sailor

Is it enough that I love you, little one, that I love your swell,
the roundness of the horizon built to contain you

and the faint ripple of your hands, little sailor. What is time
to you, who know only waves and the darkness that is

the beginning of all things. What are days when you don't
yet know breath or the press of ground under your feet.

If you are a sailor, then I am a ship whose sails flutter
as drowsing eyes are rocked to sleep by the waves.

If you are the moon, round and whole, then I am the sky
that cradles you, holding on as we inch toward morning.

Bread

I had great plans for our final morning.
I should have bought a melon and carved it
into coral crescent-moons, then prayed
and thrown the blankets out the window,

but the last thing was bread. My suitcase
poised at the door, you took bread fresh
from the paper wrapper, tore it between
your thumb and forefinger, and placed it

on my tongue. We shared such hunger,
such echoing hunger, and each bite felt
like a shadow that tasted of love that day
as crumbs fell from your callused hands.

The Visitors

My father's father was the first to appear. He said he's been at the VA
and in the attic, where time hovers beneath the eaves like sunlit dust.
I was surprised to see him so disheveled, with hair on end like feathers
and shirt cuffs open as though he hadn't seen polite company in years.

Alice visits me often these days, sometimes in a gown, sometimes a dress
that I remember from high school. She rarely speaks and won't sit still;
she is dancing or texting or talking to other people, and I wait patiently
despite the desperate want to pin her down and drink her with my eyes.

I don't mistake them for being alive, and I don't wonder why they come.
They sense my body reconfiguring, they can hear the secondary rhythm
murmuring beneath my own tired heart. My heart is full of the girl
who is not quite born, and those who are not quite gone, and I know

this is their only chance to meet in a brief, mad congress of burgeoning
and present and imagined bodies, so they may walk into my arms and
feel the ever-growing weight of her. Their stories ended but the pages
keep turning inside me; they are always welcome; I am always wanting.

Summer

I climb the wide west hill and the city
reeks of stagnant late summer: first urine
pooled under the bridge, then the dumpster
behind the Indian buffet on 21st Avenue.

Higher up on the hill, exhaust and roses
mix with the chemical stink of fertilizer
and the fumes from paint slapped onto
an apartment building's black-iron rails.

I descend to the waterfront where
the scent is late-summer blackberries
warming on the vine, eucalyptus, the faint
flintiness of soil, and oil from a docked ship.

Then I go home and eat a peach so ripe I have to close my eyes.

The Birds Have Returned from Africa

The birds have returned from Africa and tonight the flock
spins dervish-like around the hilltop church's dome.

From our window, I watch foam-colored wings churn the air
and dive away, slicing the twilight like little white knives.

I wish I could fall and feel only sky, crossing borders
with the ease of these fierce, fragile ambassadors of wind.

Later, we hear the birds call to each other, perhaps looking down
on our deliberate touch, perhaps thinking *I wish I could do that.*

I wish you weren't lost in the country of your mind
where you stay even when the weather is warm.

You are the dervish and I am the spinning—I cannot find you,
no map can help me enter the land that exists solely within you,

just you, the birds, and this beautiful night,
the sky stung with stars, knives twisted in flight.

The Last Time I Saw You

On the late walk home, we saw a man sprawled
prone and frantic, face-up on the pavement,
blood running in a thin stream from his head
to a seam in the gum-stained sidewalk.

You called 911. Patrons averted their eyes
when I asked for a stack of napkins from
the nearest restaurant. I told the man
to put pressure on the wound, he told me

to fuck off, so I uselessly clutched a handful
of napkins as the river of himself poured
into the lamp-lit street. Lights flashed,
help arrived, I held his uneven gaze.

When it was your turn a few weeks later,
who was it that stopped for you? Did they
call for help, did they hold the line during those
long, terrible minutes as traffic rushed by?

Could they see what we never saw but always
knew, how bright you were inside? Did they watch
your mouth move with each last shimmering breath;
did they think for a moment you would be saved?

Hunger

Every two hours during my daughter's first months
I settle her in the curve of a pillow and open myself.

A sting like sleeping flesh reanimating, then milk swells
from my shoulders and beneath my knees, pouring

into her, a river awakened by her sharp, barking whine.
It is night, my eyes are gritty. It is day, my shadow slants

against the stark living room wall. When I try to stand,
she reaches for me again, forming to me, her mouth

buried and adhered as milk bubbles at its corners.
I hold her until her eyes close and my wrist buckles.

Gods and Fathers

I'm sure his hands cupped my shoulders.

I'm sure my dad smiled at me and lifted me up
and held me against him the length of a breath.

I'm sure he pressed his cheek against mine
and broke my Cheerios in half,
but I don't remember any of it.

In the ancient days, fathers had stones
and whittled spears and fire,
elements of a brutal world laid bare.

The gods lived up on the mountain,
which was conveniently too high to climb
to ask for their unreliable benevolence.

Was I ever enough, laid out naked and new,
blank and needy and desperate?

My dad still can't hear me when I call,

he belongs on the mountain with the gods
and goats and tiny purple flowers,
powerful and distant and unimpressed.

I'm sure he wiped a fleck of dust from my eye.
If only I could remember, if only my voice could
reach that far or my legs climb that high.

Prayer

I live on a city block under blue sky and vermillion
and crimson trees in the same aching world as you

but on opposite shores that feel as distant as
they are. I kneel down and kiss the ground,

I kiss my daughter's face that smells of milk
and tears, and I taste the quiet salt that remains.

And if I speak to my god, what can I say when
so much of the world is on fire and my daughter

sleeps curled on her side like a solitary prawn?
I might say, why did you make my hands so small

and the oceans so wide? I might give thanks
that suffering is bundled into billions of tiny parcels

that we carry on our backs like tired hobos
riding the rails. I might say, put those sad stories

back in your mouth—except for the room
where my daughter sleeps, the rest can burn.

In Praise of Fat Babies

To approximate a baby's skin,
round your palm over a puff of kinky moss
latched low and tight against the dirt,
or press your thumb against a Northwest jellyfish,
clear and firm and innocuous as aspic.

It is difficult to describe flesh
except in terms of flesh.
My daughter's cheek overflows her jawline.
Other babies have plump arms and legs
like they are wearing doughnuts for garters.

What a relief when they eat well,
when they nurse so hard your heart
alters its syncopation,
when they rake their fingers around their plate,
rooting through traces of strawberries and toast.

Feeling the warm heft of my daughter's thigh,
I remember a bar just outside Avignon
where a ham hock wrapped in a red-checked
cheesecloth rested in a cardboard box,
out in the open, skin on, hoof intact.

Lucky Girl

Before our German Shepherd was spayed
my parents tied her to our swing set
during heat and my sister and I took turns
watching her to keep the boy dogs away.

I was lucky that no dogs came near
as she paced in circles around the slide,
fluid dripping onto the green clipped grass.
I was lucky on many other occasions—

the time in college when a man
on a bicycle grabbed me from behind
as I walked through the dove-gray night
from play rehearsal to my house

or the time a man blocked the exit
at the top of the subway stairs
and pulled his dick out of his pants
and asked me in French if I liked it

or the time I fought off my boss
as his lips smeared down my neck,
and the whole next day I had to
talk myself out of throwing up.

As a child, I didn't realize that I was just
another girl-dog tied up with rope,
and luck would dictate the slack in the line
and what beasts would enter the yard.

Flourishing Desert

The Cascades grew out of
millions of years of attrition.

I think of this while watching
my husband hang streamers for a party—

the streams and forests and canyons
are decorations, and we are guests

who come late and tap the keg
before setting the house on fire.

Flowers are blooming
out of season,

covering the desert
with gentle mallow.

Age of water, age of dust.
We travel on bones.

Under the market's fluorescent lights,
I hold an apple to my daughter's nose

and she smiles the whole length
of her gums, as if to say

this ephemera is so delicious,
I don't *care* if it lasts.

Ants

Late spring, and already the third infestation.
Today ants arrive from a gap in the garage wall
and parade along dark floorboards to the kitchen.

I nurse my daughter on the couch while ants
swarm up the counter, pacing around plates,
climbing the sides of an abandoned glass.

Of course we love our children; of course we are
savages. Spoonfuls of Borax are stirred into a bowl
of honey then dotted onto foil and placed around

the room, sweet and slightly grainy like Ovaltine
drunk warm before bed. I nurse my daughter
as ants pour in from the wall, their bodies

iridescent as black pearls. They call their friends
in inaudible voices to come and share this feast,
to store the crumbs and grow their babies strong.

Betrayal

Just before impact
a bird cries to the window,
I thought you were sky!

The Drive

At the beginning of the road is home—
stretches of dark water, the cries of gulls

and pieces of your childhood that are sealed
in our hands for safekeeping, smooth and

round like palm-warmed pebbles gathered
from the beach. Your car carries you south,

past trees and undulating grass and fences,
past malls and shops with glowing red signs.

We are not the driver.
We are not your passengers.

Think of us as a benevolent landscape
as you drive, like trees lining the road,

part of you as the breath in your lungs,
as the river below that softly fills its bed.

One black barge floats down the river
as your car skims along damp asphalt.

The radio gently and somberly
speaks the news of the world.

You are still in the twilight; one hand grips
the wheel, one hand falls slack at your side.

Your chest rises and falls like a carousel
as the sun lapses behind the trees.

At the end of the road is another home—
the school, swifts, and cooking pots,

and porch lights on the hill. The bridge
is sound as you cross the swollen river.

It is almost night, but not quite—the trees
are dark against glowing houses,

the sky is pink and gray like a sea-rinsed shell
resting on a rainy northern beach.

Two headlights shine clear into the night,
pointing west, now slowing as a light rain falls.

If I ever allege you don't understand me, know—

If I am a loose sheet of music where the notes
scurry down the bass clef like a troop of tiny ants,
then you are the accompanist who pounds the keys,
reading each note from behind coke-bottle glasses.

If I am a cardboard advent calendar covered in sky
and the pixilated faces of the holy family, then you
are the one whose nails can slip behind the flimsy
perforated edge, opening it to reveal a tiny star.

If I am the girl with the menu, then you are the pen
in the waiter's pocket, you are the chef's hands,
his knife as it rocks through a sheaf of parsley,
you are the plate, the steam that rises to my face.

Tour Guide

Your mother walks toward you
and because of the tilt of the sun
you can't see if she is happy or sad.

You don't need to see her face.
It is the rise of her shoulders
and the set of her jaw cast in shadow

as she walks along the beach
below your grandparents' house
that tells you she is a tour guide

in the land of breath, she is
thinking of them sitting upstairs
waiting for her to bring the dinner trays.

What Dying is Like

The last time your parents carry you sleeping
through the damp night to the car

and rest you in the backseat, your cheek
sticky against the leather.

They speak in low tones as you
breathe dreamlessly

under the haze of golden headlights
that paint your skin.

The world is already different
when they lift you

in the hollows of their arms
and carry you upstairs,

hours before the streetlights dim
and the sky lights itself on fire,

before you wake alone, still in your clothes,
to find that morning has crept in

unnoticed and soaked you in a pool
of soft white light.

Baby Talks

The bars around me glow
white as teeth. My stomach
feels cold and chalky like
a stretch of high desert

dappled by the shadows
of an unhurried moon.
I'm lost as loose pennies
tossed into a fountain.

Then arms lift me like ropes
winching a stalled car
from a glacial lake
blue under mountain sky.

This is what Earth must feel
each morning when it turns
to face the sun—recognition,
warmth in my mouth,

passing into my body
like light. Now is
the peace of suspension,
the perpetual turn,

and I know and don't know
that all is well
as it could ever be—
this moment of rest

when my head meets
the chest, so I do it over
and over again, one side
then the other, sigh after sigh.

Rocking Chair at the End of the World

All I want at the end of the world is to hold you
like I do now, your convex form heavy in sleep,
if there is a body to bend in the world beyond

the world. What form will we take when life
is just the memory of a wave that has crested
and slipped back beneath the dark, still water?

Will we find each other in this faceless buoyancy
and assemble like spokes on a wheel,
spinning our communal weightlessness?

The world will howl at you, little one, and the rest
is a mystery, for now. For now, sink into me and
we will rest, your cheek in the curve of my neck,

your chest draped over mine. I'll wait for you
while your delicate density is suspended in sleep,
I'll hold you outside of time, outside of breath.

In Good Voice

There is room in the world for all things,
for the sunrise staining east-facing windows,

for numbers filling the spreadsheets
on every computer,

for dirt kicked up on unpaved roads,
a lonely tin mailbox dented on one side,

for babies growing in teardrop bellies,
and the boy whose nose is flattened against the school bus window.

There is room for missing socks,
slumped and dusty in God's dark corners,

for paper clips,
the ponytail holders you wore on your wrist,

for handfuls of confetti tossed in a parade,
avocado peels curling in as they dry like tiny leather canoes,

for rivers running with sapphire dye,
coastal French towns whose names end in *sur-Mer*,

for a hundred black suitcases riding the revolving belt,
for hands that pluck guitar chords badly,

and my childhood singing teacher who stood blond
and barrel-chested with his arms out wide

and said, "I hope you have come in good voice."
There is room for all my days, and yours, dust

trapped between the wood slats of the windows
of your life and pulled taut by a single white string.

Sarah Bokich is a writer and marketing consultant. She received her BA from the University of Portland, and her MBA from Portland State University. Her work has appeared in *VoiceCatcher, Cloudbank,* and *The Timberline Review.* Sarah lives with her husband and daughter in Portland, Oregon. She can be contacted at www.sarahbokich.com.

www.ingramcontent.com/pod-product-compliance
Lightning Source LLC
LaVergne TN
LVHW041520070426
835507LV00012B/1698